Drink The Tea:
A Beginner's Guide and Journal

Vivian Caethe

PHOTOGRAPHS BY Amber Peter

ISBN: 1490512896
ISBN-13: 978-1490512891

Designed and typeset by Amber Peter

DEDICATION

To mom, for introducing me to tea

TABLE OF CONTENTS

Step One: Drink the Tea · 1

Part One

What is Tea? · 5

A (Very) Brief History of Tea · 7

Tea Bags and Iced Tea · 18

Tea: Where It Comes From, How It's Made · 21

Part Two

The Six Classes of Tea · 26

Part Three

How to Buy Tea · 46

Preparing Your Tea · 48

Putting Stuff in your Tea · 50

Storing and Caring for Your Tea · 52

Tea Parties and Afternoon Tea · 53

Yixing Taepots and Gaiwans · 56

A Few Final Notes · 58

Tea Journal · 59

Recommended Reading · 97

References · 99

Endnotes · 102

Image Information · 106

About the Author · 109

About the Photographer · 109

ACKNOWLEDGMENTS

First off, I would like to acknowledge my photographer, Amber Peter, for her work and dedication to this process. I could not have done this without my editors, nor the support of my loving husband. To all of you, thank you and drink the tea.

It was all very well to say "Drink me," but the wise little Alice was not going to do that in a hurry: "no, I'll look first," she said "and see whether it's marked 'poison' or not"… However, this bottle was not marked "poison," so Alice ventured to taste it, and finding it very nice... she very soon finished it off.

– Lewis Carrol

STEP ONE: DRINK THE TEA

The world of tea can sometimes be intimidating, bringing forth images of high class snobbery, old ladies with frumpy hats, and rituals with exacting rules and oftentimes obscure particulars.

Some of the questions I get asked the most often are those that deal with the hows, whys, and wherefores of tea drinking. How do you drink green tea? When do you put milk in your tea? Why does the pinkie go up? Who drinks tea? What do the different teas taste like? Where does a particular tea come from?

Unless you are prepared to begin experimenting, or if you are so lucky as to have a friend or family member with some experience, tea can be unapproachable. With the classes, styles, types and blends, it is possible for a beginner to become overwhelmed with the sheer variety.

However, with the exception of water, tea is the most widely consumed beverage in the world. "It is the only beverage commonly served hot or iced, anytime, anywhere, for any occasion.".[1]

Tea carries with it the history of the world. Every sip every person in the world takes every day is filled with the history and culture that conspire to bring that particular tea to their table. Each cup tells the story of the land that grew the plant and the people who plucked the leaves. The story can start in hand-picked tea from a high mountainous garden in China, it can start in the sustainable tea farms in Kenya, or it could start even in the United States, where tea has been grown since the Revolutionary War.[2]

By knowing the trappings and rituals of tea, you can begin to understand the cultural and historical aspects, but they are not necessary to enjoy your first cup. Tea has the strength to stand on its own. The history and traditions, while important, are not vital to the initial experience. Those things can come later with knowledge and experience and will often enhance the learning process as you journey deeper into tea.

Sound intimidating? It shouldn't, because you are now part of that process. By buying tea and reading this book you have become a part of its worldwide journey, the final component in the life cycle of the humble tea leaf.

That being said, if you are reading this, it may be safe to assume a more than passing interest in tea. If you are just beginning your tea adventure, welcome. And if you are already familiar with tea, it is our hope that this book will serve to enhance your tea experience. Either way, I hope this book will further drive you to learn more about tea and its history, taste, and culture.

This book is meant as a guide to the world of tea and it shouldn't be considered the end-all-be-all list of commandments about tea. Rather, this book is merely a guide to the very basics of all that tea is and can be. This book is comprised of two halves. The first half is made of three parts. The first part incorporates the history and basics about tea and tea processing. The second discusses tea itself. Finally, the third discusses how to buy tea, how to take tea, and other factors of tea culture. The second half is a journal in which you can record your experiences with tea and track your tea journey.

Finally, it should be assumed, unless stated otherwise, that every time "tea" is mentioned the word refers to loose leaf tea. This is partly to avoid confusion but also because loose leaf is by far the superior form of tea, usually sourced from either whole or larger parts of leaves. In contrast, tea bags often use lower quality leaves.

With these tools, you will embark upon a tea journey that I hope will be the first step toward a lifetime of exploration and enjoyment.

So, drink the tea.

PART ONE

It has been well said that tea is suggestive of a thousand wants, from which spring the decencies and luxuries of civilization.

— Agnes Repplier

WHAT IS TEA?
OR, FIRST SOME NOMENCLATURE

The *Camellia sinesis* plant is the source of all true tea. Served hot or cold, tea is only tea if it comes from the tea plant itself.

Although tea is made from leaves, many times people forget that tea actually comes from a real plant that grows in the ground and has real leaves instead of tiny labeled tea bags. However it is an evergreen shrub that can grow to over ten feet if left to its own devices. Nestling close to the stem, the small white flowers have large yellow stamens characteristic of other camellia plants[3].

The appropriate term for non-*Camellia sinesis* drinks commonly referred to as tea is *tisane*. This word refers to any other infusion of plant material in water to create a beverage for consumable purposes.

This means that, to people who tend to be particular about their terminology, there is no such thing as "peppermint tea".

Tisanes are often used as soothing drinks and sleep aids due to their warmth and lack of caffeine. Chamomile, for instance, is considered to have a soporific effect, while mint in its varieties is known to calm stomachs and reduce digestive disturbances.

There are four common types of drinks that are generically referred to as tea:

- Tea
- Herbal Tisanes
- Rooibos
- Yerba Mate

Of these four, only tea comes from the *Camellia sinesis* plant. Herbal tisanes come from a variety of plants, from the above peppermint and chamomile to hibiscus, dried fruit, rose hips, lemon grass and other such ingredients. Rooibos comes from a South African bush *Aspalathus linearis*, and Yerba Mate comes from the *Ilex paraguariensis* plant, which is related to the holly plant.

A (VERY) BRIEF HISTORY OF TEA

The ways that the *Camellia Sinensis* plant can be prepared gives breadth and depth of variety to the beverage, spanning from green to black teas with a universe of flavors and choices. Some scholars believe that in its most basic form, tea has been a beverage of choice for humans since before 1,000 BCE.[4] But it took hundreds of years for humans to discover all the ways that it can be treated to draw out the multitude of flavor profiles and classes that we have today.

Called cha, te, chai, and tea, among many of its names, tea is a truly international drink. It spans centuries and continents with its escapades and adventures.

The origins of this amazing drink lie with what is thought to be a happy accident. The legend goes that sometime around 2700 BCE the Emperor Shen Nong commanded that all his subjects boil their water before drinking it for good health. While doing so himself, several leaves from the nearby tea plant fell into his pot. The resulting smell so enticed him that he tasted the liquid and decided that it was delicious.[5] In other stories related to Shen Nong and tea, it is said that the famous second emperor decided to taste one hundred plants to see what they would do. Most of them made him sick, but only one of them made this sickness go away: tea.[6] And so tea became joined in the minds of the people with the riches of the aristocracy.

Due to the caffeine content, taste, and ease of preparation and transport, tea transformed from more than just a commodity to a currency. Tea, as with all precious commodities, was soon traded for goods and services. In the seventh century, a princess who married the king of Tibet in the seventh century brought with her silkworm eggs, tea, and Buddhism, thus converting an entire country not only to a new religion but also a new addiction.[7]

Around this time period, tea had made its way across Asia. Bricks of the broken remnants of tea were used to trade for horses and purchase goods, which led to the creation of the Tea Horse Road, a trade route between China and Nepal that would last long into the twentieth century.[8]

This trade, for horses on the Chinese end of the road, and for tea on the Tibetan was not only mutually beneficial, it was vital to the Chinese interests. China had a lot of tea, which wouldn't grow in Tibet. On the other hand, Tibet had a lot of horses, and the Chinese were never able to raise horses of their own that weren't weak and scrawny. To make matters worse, the Chinese desperately needed horses because the Mongols had them and it was all but impossible for the Chinese to defeat the hordes while on foot. The problem was that when the Mongols got a taste for tea, they wanted more, and the best way to do that was to pillage and then eventually take over

whole parts of Asia, including China. So to forestall this, the Chinese traded tea for horses.[9]

But in times of peace, the Chinese traded in tea, silk and other goods with other nations, such as Persia and even parts of Africa. Tea came to the Middle East and other parts of Eurasia in or around the 7th century with the trade routes of the Tang dynasty, known as the Silk Road. The Islamic countries, in particular, were fond of tea because it was not alcohol and provided a stimulating effect rather than a dampening one. With their religious beliefs that forbade alcohol, the Muslims went for tea in a big way, turning it into a strong, flavored drink with herbs and spices or sweetened with mint, as in the case of Moroccan tea.

Tea culture blossomed and bloomed throughout Eurasia, radiating from China like the fine blooms of the tea plant. Poets and artists composed works dedicated to tea. Lu Yu wrote the *Cha Ching*, the first whole book about tea in the 700s. He is quoted as writing

that "The effect of tea is cooling and as a beverage it is most suitable. It is especially fitting for persons of self-restraint and inner worth."[10] His book, the first and most comprehensive for centuries, detailed every aspect of tea production and enjoyment.[11]

As with the Chinese princess, religion helped the spread of tea to Japan in the twelfth century, where Buddhist monks who had gone to China to study came back with the delightful drink that had amazing health properties and contributed to the spirituality of the drinker. However tea drinking didn't really catch on until the 15th century with the re-introduction of tea by a monk named Shukō, who invented the tea ceremony.[12]

However as the years passed, the Japanese didn't just stop with drinking tea in the simple tea ritual invented by Shukō. They turned it into a ritual with over a hundred different utensils and equipment (called dōgu) used in close to a thousand movements and protocols throughout the duration of the tea ceremony.[13]

In addition to this ritual, the Japanese had tea identifying contests in which the host provided ten kinds of tea for the guests to sample blind. The guest who was able to identify more of the tea than anyone else was declared the victor. These tea contests were so popular that they quickly became identified with licentiousness and gluttony as they turned into raucous parties with banquets and wanton women. Needless to say, there were many people who looked down on these tea celebrations and thought them wasteful and not in keeping with the true spirit of tea.[14] Lu Yu would have been quite disappointed in them.

Another person who was disappointed in the extravagant tea culture was Sen no Rikyū in the 16th century. During this time, people were building tea ceremony houses out of gold and hoarding priceless tea utensils.[15] Tea ceremonies had become more than a peaceful get together with friends, but a full-blown social occasion. Rikyū decided to have none of that and introduced the concepts of *wabi* and *sabi* to the Japanese tea culture. These concepts, when combined, imply simplicity and the contemplation of the worth of the old and faded.[16] A return to simpler times where nature and

natural progressions held sway and people sought inner quietude and peace when they got together to drink tea.

Rikyū is famously quoted as saying "The Way of Tea is naught but this: first you boil water, then you make the tea and drink it."[17] His tea ceremonies were known for being simple and contemplative, with few of the extravagant trappings of his contemporary teadrinkers. As he gathered a following, the tea ceremony transformed to encompass and treasure the humble, becoming less excessive and more in tune with the concepts of *wabi* and *sabi*.

Additionally, the 17th century brought about innovations with loose leaf tea that transformed the tea drinking experience. Prior to this, tea was dried, pressed into cakes and made ready to transport.

When someone wanted a cup of tea, they had to crush the cake, grind it into a powder, sift it, place it in a bowl, add hot water and whisk it into a frothy drink. Thus the requisite tea utensils were a source of hot water, a whisk, a wide cup (to allow for the whisking motion) and a grinder.[18] However, this process relied on a style of tea called "wax tea" in which fresh leaves were put through a complex process by which little stamped cakes were made. The Emperor loved it, and so did everyone else.

The problem was that this manufacturing and consuming process was expensive and everyone wanted to be able to drink tea. In response to this, the modern means of making the different kinds of tea were developed by trial and error, leading to the six classes of tea that we have today. Among these were the highly-prized oolongs that people began to love simply because of the complex flavors that could be brought forth through the way the tea was picked, dried and prepared.[19]

Because of this, loose leaf tea became more popular and the teapot was invented as a means to infuse the tea with hot water and then serve it. Some of the most famous tea pots are known as Yixing tea pots due to the location of the clay from which they are made.

The innovations in tea production that developed oolong and black teas also made the tea trade with the Middle East and Europe blossom into a full-blown industry. Green tea, which could not be stored for long periods of time, was replaced for commerce with travel-hardy black tea.[20]

The story behind Russian Caravan tea is exemplary of the tea trade and the innovations which marked its movement out of Asia and into Europe. In the 15th century, tea made it's great debut in Russia, a country known for its strong teas and a unique tea innovation called the *samovar*. But in order to get tea from China to Russia, merchants and caravans were forced to cross rough and rugged terrain between the two countries. This journey took over a year and made the tea a near-priceless commodity affordable only by the rich and the royal.[21]

Legend has it that the smoked Russian Caravan tea received its distinct taste through being stored by the campfires of such caravans on their long journeys through the wastes and mountains to bring precious Chinese goods to avid Russian customers.

Once the tea did get to Russia, the Russians promptly invented the *samovar*, or their response to the Chinese tea pot. According to some, the samovar was invented by a Russian gunsmith, Fedor Lisitsin and his two sons, who, when not making guns, spent their time perfecting their invention.[22] Not only did it brew tea, it also heated it by having a small boiler in the base that allowed the tea to remain brewing and heated. The samovar became not only a vital component to everyday Russian life, but also the prized centerpiece of any Russian household.[23]

Now that it had spread from China, to the Middle East, Africa, parts of Europe, and then to Russia, tea finally came to England. This did not happen, however until the 1600s after the marriage of Charles II and the Portuguese Catherine of Braganza.[24]

During this time, the East India Company was formed to import the riches of the East to England. Since the sun never set on the British Empire, tea spread with the British to the rest of the world, including the Americas and to American culture. Tea was so prized by Americans that its taxation led to one of the most familiar instances of American tea-related history: the Boston Tea Party. [25] Others have pointed to this unfortunate incident as proof that Americans are bad at making tea.[26]

Acerbations aside, the British were not only good at making tea; they were also good at making empires. The East India Company would have a two hundred year monopoly on the tea trade with China, but when its total control over the tea market was threatened by American interests as well as an increasing Chinese hostility toward the British, the East India Company sent forth Robert Fortune to steal the plants from China and import them to India.[27]

But this was no easy task. The problem lay in the fact that the tea plant, while hardy in its natural environment, is tricky to

transplant. Not only did the British have to steal the plant from the Chinese farmers, a daunting prospect in itself, but they also had to find a way to make it grow outside its natural environment. Attempts to grow it in England itself resulted in failure.

Robert Fortune, however, had a plan. Through his other sojourns into Chinese territory to examine and gain samples of the indigenous plants, he had become adept at disguising himself as a Chinese merchant. Taking with him boxes especially designed to transport plants, he ventured forth into the deepest parts of China, places where no Englishman had been allowed before.[28]

After what had to be a heart pounding transaction where he purchased tea plants from unwitting Chinese farmers, he smuggled them up the river and to the port. Undoubtedly he was sure he would be caught at any moment, and it is left to the reader to wonder how he felt as he traversed the immense countryside with his stolen crate of priceless tea plants.

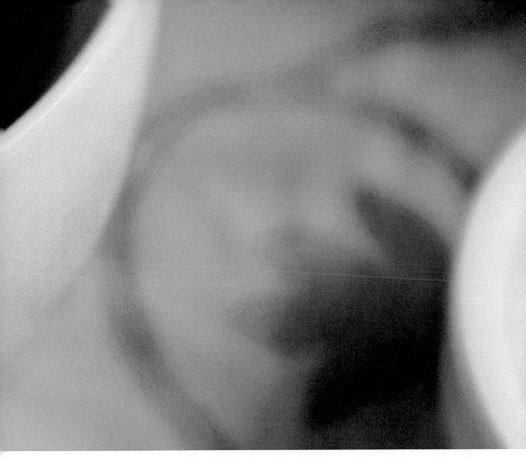

Only when Robert Fortune successfully smuggled seeds from China and into India in the mid-1880's did the British manage to plant them in Darjeeling, where they took root as the first tea plants completely controlled by the East India Company.[29]

Decades passed and the East India Company fell, but tea production did not decline. Tea had set its roots in the world. Even the United States, with its notorious fascination with coffee, had a soft spot in its collective heart for tea. By the 1970s, when China reopened exports to the United States, fine tea had its revival in America.[30]

From its early origins as a few leaves in a pot of water to a worldwide drink of choice, tea has spread to hundreds of countries where tea is grown even today. However with all its breadth and availability, the majority of the world's tea comes from four countries: China, India, Kenya and Sri Lanka.[31]

TEA BAGS AND ICED TEA
OR, A FEW NOTES ON AMERICAN TEA

Tea bags and iced tea are the two ways in which most Americans are introduced to the world of tea. Often sweetened or served with a bag in a tiny stainless steel teapot in restaurants throughout the country, most Americans rarely think about the origins of this illustrious drink.

Although it is considered a predominantly British affectation in the modern United States, some of the innovations in tea technology are actually American.

For example, tea bags were invented accidentally by a New York tea purveyor by the name of Thomas Sullivan. When he sent samples of tea to his customers, he used small silk bags to package them. When they received the small sachets, the customers thought they were meant to be used in the manner we use tea bags today, and thus the tea bag was born.[32]

Eighty five percent of all tea consumed by Americans is iced. [33] Along with tea bags, iced tea is predominantly an American invention. Its commercial iteration was first popularized at the 1904 World's Fair and caught on with the increased accessibility of refrigeration.[34]

Iced tea has been a popular drink ever since the green tea-based "punches" of the 1800s.[35] And as different as both are culturally, common Southern sweet tea and Northern unsweetened tea both rely on commercialized tea for their flavor.

One common quality that commercialized tea possesses is that these black teas all taste the same day after day and year after year. This is because each company creates their teas from a highly regulated blend of black teas from around the world sourced to provide a consistent taste profile with every cup. It's supposed to taste the same and so it does.[36]

This generality serves the companies that mass produce tea and is good for the general public who want their tea to be predictable in large quantities. However, it makes it a rather bland drink over time, especially if less than quality leaves are used in their production. Additionally, the generality of commercialized tea reduces overall depth and breadth of tastes and scents available in the world of teas to a single common flavor.

Comparing these teas to high quality hand-picked tea is like comparing boxed wine to Dom Pérignon. Not only is the manufacture and quality vastly different, but you might not even be talking about the same sort of thing, since often comparisons are made between classes of teas or teas and tisanes.

"On any given day, over 160 million Americans are drinking tea".[37]

Every tea…tells a story in the cup about the soil and air that nurtured it and the tea-making skills that transformed and shaped it.

— Mary and Robert Heiss

TEA: WHERE IT COMES FROM, HOW IT'S MADE

Tea should taste like where's from and what's been done to it, no more, no less. However, this doesn't mean that there aren't a wide range of flavors available in the variety of teas from across the world. Even if all the tea manufacturing processes were the same, and all the artisans shared the same practices, tea from different countries, provinces and even valleys would taste different due to the *terroir* of the tea.

Terroir is a term that comes from wine making and refers to the topography, soil, ecosystem, weather and a hundred other factors that make a specific wine from a specific area have certain taste qualities and profiles. This applies directly to tea, as the terroir of a tea can influence the complexities and distinctive flavors of the leaves.

The varieties of terroirs that are afforded by the landscapes in which tea can be grown lend themselves to hundreds of tastes and aromas. This is why teas from India are distinctive from teas from Taiwan, both of which are quite different from the variety of teas from various parts of China.[38] It is why there is such a marked flavor difference between Chinese green tea and Japanese green tea.[39]

The process by which each tea is produced also influences the taste of each tea. After harvesting, green teas are treated differently than black teas, leading to different levels of oxidation and a completely different flavor. Many of these treatments of tea, the way in which tea becomes tea, are defined by tradition and culture.

The basic means by which tea is turned from the raw leaf into a drinkable product ranges from the simplicity of white tea to the complexity of Pu-erh. Tea is processed either by machine or by hand, with higher quality teas requiring the latter treatment. There are five basic steps to making any sort of tea: withering, rolling, oxidation, drying and sorting. The duration of these steps and the way in which they are enacted determines the class of tea and the type of tea, as some processes result in a very particular type of tea, such as Gunpowder green tea, or even a whole class such as Pu-erh.[40]

Withering is basically what it sounds like. The leaves are picked, then left to wither and lose moisture.

Rolling is done either by hand or via the "Cut, tear, curl" (CTC) method, which creates a smaller grade of tea and is done via machine.[41]

Oxidation will be addressed later, but the method and duration of oxidation determines the class of tea and is often specific to not only the class, but the particular kind.

In the case of green tea, the oxidation phase is skipped altogether and instead the leaves are steamed before they rolled. This prevents oxidation from occurring and allows the tea to retain its vibrant green color.

Drying involves firing the leaves either in large pans or baskets, by rolling it or letting it air dry (as with white tea) to stop the oxidation process and 'fix' the tea so that it doesn't spoil.[42]

Finally, tea is sorted into size, or grade. Grades primarily apply to black tea, with the two basic classifications being Orthodox or CTC. From there, other grades are created ranging from whole leaf to dust. Fannings, which are graded just above dust, are typically what you find in tea bags.

You may see abbreviations such as "FTGFOP" when purchasing tea. These refer to a grading system that describes whether it's whole leaf as well as the processing and so forth. For example, the above abbreviation stands for "Fine Tippy Golden Flowery Orange

Pekoe." This means that it is the finest tea from an estate, comprised primarily of golden flowers, leaf buds and the youngest leaves. The entire grading system is quite complex and is not yet standardized, but there are several very good guides available online and in the recommended reading.[43]

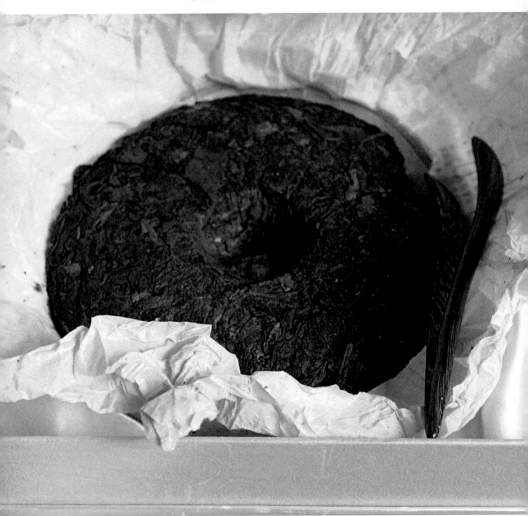

A woman is like a tea bag - you can't tell how strong she is until you put her in hot water.

— *Eleanor Roosevelt*

PART TWO

Honestly, if you're given the choice between Armageddon or tea,
you don't say 'what kind of tea?

— *Neil Gaiman*

THE SIX CLASSES OF TEA
AND VARIOUS TISANES

When discussing classes of tea, it is important to understand the concept of oxidation. While other processes previously mentioned also play a part, the level of oxidation serves as a basic distinction between the tea classes.

Oxidation, also incorrectly referred to as *fermentation*, is the chemical process by which the classes of teas are produced. The common description of oxidation is the change that occurs when an apple is sliced and then exposed to air for a period of time. This is also seen in the process whereby leaves change color in the fall. In terms of tea, the control of this oxidation differentiates the classes of tea from each other.[44]

Oxidation instills soft flavors in white tea, complex flavors in oolong and strong flavors in black teas that are distinctive to those teas. In high quality teas, these flavors are tightly controlled by the tea artisans who make each style of tea. Often, in the oldest tea manufacturing areas, this oxidation is done by feel and taste via senses honed by generations of tea making.[45]

Green and yellow teas have no oxidation, while white tea has only the natural oxidation that arises from its particular process, or lack of processing entirely. Oolong tea has the greatest range of oxidation, from fifteen to eighty percent, as determined by the artisan and process particular to oolongs. Black tea is almost completely oxidized.

Pu-erh is its own particular class of tea and has its own particular history. The only truly fermented tea, there are two different styles: *Sheng* (raw) Pu-erh and *Shou* (ripe) Pu-erh, distinguished by whether they are oxidized or not.[46]

Tisanes, as mentioned above, have no tea in them whatsoever, but these are distinct from blended and flavored teas that incorporate herbs and flavors in them. For example, Earl Grey is infused with bergamot oil, which provides it with that citrus scent. Additionally, teas like Lapsang Souchong are smoked, and have a distinctive strong campfire smell. Others have flowers in them, such as lavender or rose teas.

These blended teas and flavored teas are built for the most part on a base of black tea, although there are some exceptions. There is, for example, Genmaicha, which is a green tea with roasted rice added in, which gives it a delicious roasted taste. White teas are also sometimes enhanced with citrus or flowers to compliment the delicate flavors.

Green Tea

Oxidation: minimal

Water temperature: 170-180°F

The flavors of green tea are often described as bright, leafy, grassy, herbaceous and brisk.

After being picked, leaves for green tea are steamed, then dried and fired in a variety of methods to stop oxidation. The leaf may also be rolled, as with Gunpowder, and then tumbled to maintain the distinctive shape. Another form of green tea that is more processed than other green teas is matcha. This Japanese style of green tea is ground to a powder and then whisked. Top grade matcha is served in Japanese tea ceremonies.[47]

The water temperature for green tea is vital to note due to the fact that green tea can become bitter and quite unpleasant if it is brewed at too hot a temperature. If you are using an electric kettle without a variable temperature, the proper temperature can be achieved by dropping one to two ice cubes into the boiling water per every eight ounces.

Yellow Tea

Oxidation: partial

Water temperature: 170-180°F

The flavors of yellow tea have been described as mellower and softer than green tea, but still possessing an herbaceous flavor that keeps it from tasting too much like a white or a black tea.

Yellow tea is from only specific parts of China. The process that makes it is called *men huan* or "sealing yellow", which refers to the way it is prepared. The color of yellow tea is produced due to the artisans leaving the tea out to wither slightly longer before it is processed and fired.[48]

As with green teas, the temperature of water for yellow teas is imperative to note so as not to sear the delicate leaves.

White Tea

Oxidation: natural

Water temperature: 160-170°F

These teas have a distinctly soft and sweet flavor that brings to mind the dewy mornings of spring or such flavors as honeydew.

White tea is the least processed of all teas as the buds are only steamed before they are dried and sold. Using few to no full leaves, white tea is comprised of the first buds that bloom in the early spring and as such lend that flavor to the tea.[49]

White tea was popular among the British aristocracy in the early days of tea importation to England. It was named "Silver Tip Pekoe" by the British, who were confusing it with black tea.

Due to its delicate nature, the temperature for this tea is even lower than green or yellow teas. When preparing this tea, monitor the temperature carefully.

Oolong Tea

Oxidation: 15-80%

Water temperature: 180-200°F

Oolongs are some of the sweetest and most aromatic teas available and, due to the wide variety of ways in which they are produced, their flavor can vary across a wide spectrum of tastes.

Due to the complexity of their flavors, oolongs benefit from multiple infusions and their flavors will develop and transform over each infusion.

The most famous oolong is the Iron Goddess of Mercy tea, also known as Tieguanyin. This oolong has a round, apricot flavor that his highly prized by tea connoisseurs.

This tea is also more delicate than black teas and the water temperature should be less so as not to make the tea overly bitter and ruin the subtle flavors.

Black Tea

Oxidation: full

Water temperature: 190-200°F

Due to its almost complete oxidation, black tea has a strong, tannic flavor that is instantly recognizable. Some black teas have honey notes, and others have strong floral undertones. Others are enhanced with flavors or treatments, such as Earl Grey or Lapsang Souchong.

Accounting for seventy-five percent of all tea made in the world, black tea is also the most prevalent kind of tea in the Western world and is the most commonly seen served in Western restaurants and coffeeshops. It is also the only tea that can stand being enhanced with milk or sugar.

If overbrewed, it can become bitter and tannic. Tannins released from the oxidized leaves make the tea taste very akin to shoe leather if the leaves are steeped for too long.

Black tea has the highest caffeine levels of any tea, but due to the other components of its chemical composition, it doesn't cause the jitters.

The water temperature for black tea should be close to boiling. Due to the increased oxidation, more heat is required to release the full flavors of the tea. Depending on the tea, this tea can be infused fully at least three times for full enjoyment.

Black tea is also the most commonly flavored tea. A notable example is Earl Grey tea, which was named for Charles Grey, the Second Early Gray. Although he is more famous for the tea that was named after him than the sweeping reforms to the British Electoral system, this only came about because the Chinese bergamot tea had been gifted to him by an ambassador and he happened to like it.[50]

Pu-erh

Oxidation: either complete or none; fermented

Water temperature: 200-212°F

Pu-erh has a distinct flavor often described as earthy, reminiscent of mushrooms, damp soil, or iron. This is a tea that every connoisseur should try at least once and entire books could be devoted to its study.

While the term "fermented" is often incorrectly applied to the oxidation of other teas, it is appropriate for Pu-erh. Modern Pu-erh is the descendant of the tea cakes and bricks used for transport and sale in the early history of tea, and was discovered through a happy accident when some teas in brick form were transported down the Tea Horse Road. During this transport, some of the tea began to ferment due to the storage conditions as well as the microbes in the tea.

This created a unique form of tea with a distinctive dark red color and a round, full mouthfeel. Not only is it delicious, but it is also used as a digestive in China.

The water temperature for Pu-erh is full boiling to release the full benefit of the tea. This tea can and should be infused multiple times.

Tisanes

Oxidation: n/a

Water temperature: 200-212°F

Since tisanes are not teas, and are made from herbs or flowers, they typically can tolerate higher temperatures of water. In some cases, boiling water will be required to release the flavors of the tisanes, especially mints.

If possible, fresh tisanes are best, as they will allow the release of the oils in the leaves and create a rounder, fuller drink. However, most tisanes are available dry, such as the herbal teas made available by many tea companies.

In addition to being flavorful, some tisanes are also used medicinally. For example, chamomile is used as a relaxation and sleep aid and peppermint is useful as a stomach and nerve calmer. In Ayurvedic practices, tisanes are also tied to the chakras and are used to cleanse the spirit as well as the body.

Rooibos

Oxidation: n/a, fermented

Water temperature: 200-212°F

Rooibos is also a tisane and comes from the Aspalathus lineari bush in South Africa and its name means "red bush" in Afrikaans. It can either be prepared fermented or raw, and is referred to as either "red" or "green."[51]

There are purportedly many health benefits to drinking rooibos, among which are the effects of the antioxidants present in the tisane, much like the antioxidants in tea.

Rooibos tisanes are available in many flavors and blends, and vanilla is lauded as a delicious compliment to it. Fruit and spices are also added to this tisane to great effect.

Rooibos benefits from boiling water as well, due to its hardy nature, it takes more for the flavors to be released.

PART THREE

Teaism is a cult founded on the adoration of the beautiful among the sordid facts of everyday existence. It inculcates purity and harmony, the mystery of mutual charity, the romanticism of the social order. It is essentially a worship of the Imperfect, as it is a tender attempt to accomplish something possible in this impossible thing we know as life.

— *Kakuzō Okakura, The Book of Tea*

HOW TO BUY TEA

Now that we've covered the basics of drinking tea, it becomes important to discuss how to buy tea. While it may be possible to purchase bagged tea at your local grocery store, loose leaf tea is slightly less common. Higher-end grocery stores, carry loose leaf tea in small quantities, and this may be an excellent place to start, especially if your town or city doesn't have a local tea shop.

Another alternative is the internet, but there are several disadvantages. The optimal tea buying conditions involve being able to see, smell, and taste the tea before buying it. Not being able to examine the tea beforehand makes the buying process chancy, especially if there are no reviews of the website to tell whether it is trustworthy or not.

That being said, the best option is to find a local tea shop and go in and talk to them. If they are reputable, they will not only let you examine the tea, they will also be able to tell you its provenance and describe the flavor notes. They can also provide tips for brewing it, and what foods may complement the flavor. However, beware of tea shops that are snobby, who won't answer your questions, or who refuse to let you examine the tea before purchasing it. Likely as not, their tea is of subpar quality and if their customer service is lacking, you may not want to purchase tea from them in the first place.

When examining the tea, you should watch out for a stale, cardboard, or plastic smell. The smell of tea should make you want to drink the tea. It shouldn't smell bad, foul or otherwise weird. It should not smell of anything but tea. If it smells like another herb or food, it means that it was stored improperly and it has absorbed the smells from the nearby herbs or spices.[52]

By learning what certain teas smell like, you will also be able to identify the poor quality teas. This will be a matter of practice and experience, however, and often some small amount of trial and error. When purchasing tea for the first time, buy the smallest amount possible to ensure that you actually will like it. Make notes at the end of this book for all the teas that you buy in order to keep track of the ones you like and why. Some tea companies allow you to buy sample quantities or sample sets.

Although ordering tea online can be tricky, there are several tea companies that I recommend due to the consistent quality of their tea, as well as their dedication to tea culture and fair trade. These companies are Adagio Teas, Golden Moon Tea Company, and Rishi Tea. Adagio teas in particular provides excellent information on their tea and allows customer reviews with each kind of tea, which will help give you an idea as to whether you will enjoy a tea or not. Another tea company that provides excellent blends is Dryad Tea.

PREPARING YOUR TEA

CLASS	OXIDATION	TEMPERATURE	STEEPING TIME
Green Tea	Minimal	170-180	3 minutes
Yellow Tea	Partial	170-180	3 minutes
White Tea	Natural	160-170	1-3 minutes
Oolong Tea	15-80%	180-200	3-5 minutes
Black Tea	Full	190-200	3-5 minutes
Pu-Erh	Complete/None - Fermented	200-212	3-5 minutes

Try to avoid tea balls as much as possible, since they tend to stifle the expansion of the tea and prevent the flavors from being fully released. Teapots with either internal or external strainers or open infusers for mugs work best and can be purchased in many tea stores and via online vendors.

To serve tea in a pot, place one teaspoon of tea per guest in the pot, plus one for the pot. Allow to steep per the tea instructions and serve by pouring the tea through a strainer and into the cup.

The mug and pot that you use is mostly a matter of taste, but ceramics work better than metals, for many reasons. One is that metal conducts heat and will be hot. Another is that it will make your tea taste funny.

PUTTING STUFF IN YOUR TEA

As you may be aware, some people take their tea with milk, sugar, or lemon. However, there are particular ways to apply these tea enhancements

In China and Japan, tea is mostly served plain. In England, as most people know, tea is served with milk and sugar and is adjusted to the taste of the imbiber. In Russia, strong dark tea is served with a dollop of jam or a slice of lemon. Moroccan green tea is served with mint and a little sugar.

Milk works well with tea since it binds to the tannins and reduces the strong, bitter flavor. Lemon often compliments the

astringent flavor of some black teas, but is not recommended with smoother teas, such as an Assam.[53]

Never add milk to green or oolong tea. I highly recommend drinking them plain, due to the complexity of their flavors, but there are some who do add honey or sugar. I find that the flavors are so delicate that any additions to the drink merely make them into a muddy mess.

Black teas support and often welcome the inclusion of milk, sugar or lemon. Combining all three is not recommended because the lemon will curdle the milk. Always add the milk after the tea, otherwise you will scald the milk.

It is traditional to thinly slice the lemon and place it in your tea with a fork, allowing the lemon to infuse in the tea rather than squeezing it with your hands. While slicing it thinly, cloves can also be placed in the center of the slice to add another layer of flavor.

Honey may also be included, but combining honey with milk is not recommended. Honey with lemon, however, is delicious, especially in a particularly strong English Breakfast blend.

STORING AND CARING FOR YOUR TEA

While not as delicate as some dried goods, tea should still be stored in a cool dry place away from sunlight. Most teas can be stored up to nine months without the flavor fading. Pu-erh varieties will actually age with proper storage.

Do store your tea in an airtight container. Do not store it in the refrigerator as it will absorb the fridge smells and become unpalatable.

TEA PARTIES AND AFTERNOON TEA

Another way to try tea, and often to enjoy the entire experience of the Western tea ritual, is to find somewhere that does afternoon or high tea or to hold your own.

Historically there are three general kinds of tea gatherings in the Western world: Elevenses, Afternoon Tea, and High Tea.

Elevenses is, as you may suspect from the name, taken at eleven. This meal is more of a snack, and involves biscuits or cakes with tea.

High Tea, in contrast, was the working class meal served at a high table in the evening, also the last meal of the day taken by children. Although the name connotes a fancier meal, it speaks more to the time of day and the table, than the status of the tea.

Afternoon Tea is what Americans usually think of as High Tea. Afternoon Tea was a huge social affair in the 1800s, and involved very specific foods and modes of dress. For example, women were expected to wear an afternoon dress and a hat, which served as a wardrobe transition between the walking dress and an evening gown. As you may suspect, this was a very high class affair.

The origins of this tea lie in the early 1800s with the Anna, the seventh Duchess of Bedford and her "sinking feeling."[54] In order to combat this feeling, she began having a pot of tea with a light snack in the afternoon and later invited her aristocratic friends.

Tea time is between two and five pm, and is traditionally held at four pm. In modern Afternoon Teas, tea is served with scones, cream and jam as well as tiny sandwiches known as "savones." The

traditional sandwiches are cucumber, egg, smoked salmon, ham, and fish paste. Fruit and sponge cake may also be served.[55]

Etiquette for Afternoon Tea and similar tea parties is somewhat convoluted, but is good to know if partaking in a tea house or restaurant, or if you intend to have a formal Afternoon Tea for yourself and your guests. A basic introduction will follow, but further reading is recommended. These guidelines refer solely to the Western Afternoon Tea and not the Japanese tea service.

When you are the host, serve your guests first and inquire as to how they take their tea. If they request sugar, milk or lemon, accommodate their request when serving them.

Keep an eye on everyone's cup and inquire as to whether they would want more. Always pour tea into an empty cup and add a fresh lemon, if requested.

When stirring your tea with a small spoon, do not splash the tea or clink the spoon against the sides. When done with stirring, remove the spoon from the cup and place it on the back of the cup rather than on the front of the cup.[56]

If dressed for tea, wear a hat, but remove your gloves before drinking.

Don't raise your pinky. You'll just look silly. In the 1800s, the china was constructed so that the drinker couldn't put her finger through the handle and so the extended finger was used to balance the cup in the drinker's grasp. Modern tea cups are significantly more convenient and do not require the added balance.

There should be a variety of foods available for the tea, as mentioned above. But in modern teas, it is also important to consider the dietary restrictions of your guests and be aware that they may be vegetarian, on a gluten free diet, or otherwise require accommodations to a traditional menu. Also, if serving vegetarian food with non-vegetarian food, be very sure to use different serving platters and different preparation surfaces so as to avoid cross-contamination. It is also considered polite to provide other drinks for people who may not be able to drink caffeine, such as lemonade, cucumber water or even sangria.

In contrast to the above, Japanese Tea Ceremonies are completely different and infinitely more complex. While they are out of the scope of this book, more information can be found on them online or via the books listed in the further reading section.

YIXING TEAPOTS AND GAIWANS

The best sort of pot for black teas is a Yixing clay teapot or mug. The clay absorbs the flavor of the tea and overtime enhances the tea flavor. However, you should only use one class of tea in the teapot so as not to muddle the absorbed flavor. It is even recommended that you use only one kind of tea (such as Assam) in them, to help develop the flavor of the pot and cups. These teapots and tea sets are usually comparably priced to other tea pots and can be found at many tea purveyors.

Gaiwans are small cups with a lid and a saucer that allow the drinker to more fully enjoy the flavors of tea through small quantities. Becoming more popular at tea tastings, these handle-less cups are either used to decant tea by holding the lid in place and pouring only the liquid into another cup or to sip from directly. There is a trick to holding the lid in place while sipping, so some experimentation and experience is required.

A FEW FINAL NOTES

Loose leaf tea can, and often should, be infused multiple times. Most loose leaves will tolerate at least two infusions, and some black and oolong teas can be infused up to five times. If in doubt, experiment.

Tea leaves work as excellent fertilizer and composting them is highly recommended.

Although there are hundreds of books and websites on tea and tea drinking, the best way to learn about it is to try it for yourself. With this book, you have the basics necessary to begin your tea journey. It is my hope that this serves as a trusty guide and a comfortable companion.

Go forth and drink the tea.

TEA JOURNAL

I am a hardened and shameless tea drinker, who has for twenty years diluted his meals only with the infusion of this fascinating plant; whose kettle has scarcely time to cool; who with tea amuses the afternoon, with tea solaces the midnight, and with tea welcomes the evening.

— Samuel Johnson (1709-1784)[57]

Name:

Class/Type:

Country of Production:

Purchased at:

Purchased on:

Purchasing notes:

First tasting:

Length of infusion:

Water:

Temperature:

Teapot or cup used:

Color:

Aroma:

Taste:

Notes:

Name:

Class/Type:

Country of Production:

Purchased at:

Purchased on:

Purchasing notes:

First tasting:

Length of infusion:

Water:

Temperature:

Teapot or cup used:

Color:

Aroma:

Taste:

Notes:

Name:

Class/Type:

Country of Production:

Purchased at:

Purchased on:

Purchasing notes:

First tasting:

Length of infusion:

Water:

Temperature:

Teapot or cup used:

Color:

Aroma:

Taste:

Notes:

Name:

Class/Type:

Country of Production:

Purchased at:

Purchased on:

Purchasing notes:

First tasting:

Length of infusion:

Water:

Temperature:

Teapot or cup used:

Color:

Aroma:

Taste:

Notes:

Name:

Class/Type:

Country of Production:

Purchased at:

Purchased on:

Purchasing notes:

First tasting:

Length of infusion:

Water:

Temperature:

Teapot or cup used:

Color:

Aroma:

Taste:

Notes:

Name:

Class/Type:

Country of Production:

Purchased at:

Purchased on:

Purchasing notes:

First tasting:

Length of infusion:

Water:

Temperature:

Teapot or cup used:

Color:

Aroma:

Taste:

Notes:

Name:

Class/Type:

Country of Production:

Purchased at:

Purchased on:

Purchasing notes:

First tasting:

Length of infusion:

Water:

Temperature:

Teapot or cup used:

Color:

Aroma:

Taste:

Notes:

Name:

Class/Type:

Country of Production:

Purchased at:

Purchased on:

Purchasing notes:

First tasting:

Length of infusion:

Water:

Temperature:

Teapot or cup used:

Color:

Aroma:

Taste:

Notes:

Name:

Class/Type:

Country of Production:

Purchased at:

Purchased on:

Purchasing notes:

First tasting:

Length of infusion:

Water:

Temperature:

Teapot or cup used:

Color:

Aroma:

Taste:

Notes:

Name:

Class/Type:

Country of Production:

Purchased at:

Purchased on:

Purchasing notes:

First tasting:

Length of infusion:

Water:

Temperature:

Teapot or cup used:

Color:

Aroma:

Taste:

Notes:

Name:

Class/Type:

Country of Production:

Purchased at:

Purchased on:

Purchasing notes:

First tasting:

Length of infusion:

Water:

Temperature:

Teapot or cup used:

Color:

Aroma:

Taste:

Notes:

Name:

Class/Type:

Country of Production:

Purchased at:

Purchased on:

Purchasing notes:

First tasting:

Length of infusion:

Water:

Temperature:

Teapot or cup used:

Color:

Aroma:

Taste:

Notes:

Name:

Class/Type:

Country of Production:

Purchased at:

Purchased on:

Purchasing notes:

First tasting:

Length of infusion:

Water:

Temperature:

Teapot or cup used:

Color:

Aroma:

Taste:

Notes:

Name:

Class/Type:

Country of Production:

Purchased at:

Purchased on:

Purchasing notes:

First tasting:

Length of infusion:

Water:

Temperature:

Teapot or cup used:

Color:

Aroma:

Taste:

Notes:

Name:

Class/Type:

Country of Production:

Purchased at:

Purchased on:

Purchasing notes:

First tasting:

Length of infusion:

Water:

Temperature:

Teapot or cup used:

Color:

Aroma:

Taste:

Notes:

Name:

Class/Type:

Country of Production:

Purchased at:

Purchased on:

Purchasing notes:

First tasting:

Length of infusion:

Water:

Temperature:

Teapot or cup used:

Color:

Aroma:

Taste:

Notes:

Name:

Class/Type:

Country of Production:

Purchased at:

Purchased on:

Purchasing notes:

First tasting:

Length of infusion:

Water:

Temperature:

Teapot or cup used:

Color:

Aroma:

Taste:

Notes:

Name:

Class/Type:

Country of Production:

Purchased at:

Purchased on:

Purchasing notes:

First tasting:

Length of infusion:

Water:

Temperature:

Teapot or cup used:

Color:

Aroma:

Taste:

Notes:

Name:

Class/Type:

Country of Production:

Purchased at:

Purchased on:

Purchasing notes:

First tasting:

Length of infusion:

Water:

Temperature:

Teapot or cup used:

Color:

Aroma:

Taste:

Notes:

Name:

Class/Type:

Country of Production:

Purchased at:

Purchased on:

Purchasing notes:

First tasting:

Length of infusion:

Water:

Temperature:

Teapot or cup used:

Color:

Aroma:

Taste:

Notes:

Name:

Class/Type:

Country of Production:

Purchased at:

Purchased on:

Purchasing notes:

First tasting:

Length of infusion:

Water:

Temperature:

Teapot or cup used:

Color:

Aroma:

Taste:

Notes:

Name:

Class/Type:

Country of Production:

Purchased at:

Purchased on:

Purchasing notes:

First tasting:

Length of infusion:

Water:

Temperature:

Teapot or cup used:

Color:

Aroma:

Taste:

Notes:

Name:

Class/Type:

Country of Production:

Purchased at:

Purchased on:

Purchasing notes:

First tasting:

Length of infusion:

Water:

Temperature:

Teapot or cup used:

Color:

Aroma:

Taste:

Notes:

Name:

Class/Type:

Country of Production:

Purchased at:

Purchased on:

Purchasing notes:

First tasting:

Length of infusion:

Water:

Temperature:

Teapot or cup used:

Color:

Aroma:

Taste:

Notes:

Name:

Class/Type:

Country of Production:

Purchased at:

Purchased on:

Purchasing notes:

First tasting:

Length of infusion:

Water:

Temperature:

Teapot or cup used:

Color:

Aroma:

Taste:

Notes:

Name:

Class/Type:

Country of Production:

Purchased at:

Purchased on:

Purchasing notes:

First tasting:

Length of infusion:

Water:

Temperature:

Teapot or cup used:

Color:

Aroma:

Taste:

Notes:

Name:

Class/Type:

Country of Production:

Purchased at:

Purchased on:

Purchasing notes:

First tasting:

Length of infusion:

Water:

Temperature:

Teapot or cup used:

Color:

Aroma:

Taste:

Notes:

Name:

Class/Type:

Country of Production:

Purchased at:

Purchased on:

Purchasing notes:

First tasting:

Length of infusion:

Water:

Temperature:

Teapot or cup used:

Color:

Aroma:

Taste:

Notes:

Name:

Class/Type:

Country of Production:

Purchased at:

Purchased on:

Purchasing notes:

First tasting:

Length of infusion:

Water:

Temperature:

Teapot or cup used:

Color:

Aroma:

Taste:

Notes:

Name:

Class/Type:

Country of Production:

Purchased at:

Purchased on:

Purchasing notes:

First tasting:

Length of infusion:

Water:

Temperature:

Teapot or cup used:

Color:

Aroma:

Taste:

Notes:

Name:

Class/Type:

Country of Production:

Purchased at:

Purchased on:

Purchasing notes:

First tasting:

Length of infusion:

Water:

Temperature:

Teapot or cup used:

Color:

Aroma:

Taste:

Notes:

Name:

Class/Type:

Country of Production:

Purchased at:

Purchased on:

Purchasing notes:

First tasting:

Length of infusion:

Water:

Temperature:

Teapot or cup used:

Color:

Aroma:

Taste:

Notes:

Name:

Class/Type:

Country of Production:

Purchased at:

Purchased on:

Purchasing notes:

First tasting:

Length of infusion:

Water:

Temperature:

Teapot or cup used:

Color:

Aroma:

Taste:

Notes:

TEA PROVENDERS

Name	Location	Rating

FAVORITE TEAS

Place Purchased	Review Page No.	Notes

RECOMMENDED READING

The Hitchhiker's Guide to the Galaxy – Douglas Adams

The Tea Enthusiast's Handbook – Mary Lou Heiss and Robert J. Heiss.

Tea & Etiquette: Taking Tea for Business and Pleasure – Dorothea Johnson and Bruce Richardson

The Book of Tea – Kakuzō Okakura

The Tea Ceremony – Seno Tanaka, Sendo Tanaka, and Edwin O. Reischauer.

The True History of Tea – Victor H. Mair and Erling Hoh

For All the Tea in China – Sarah Rose

"I say let the world go to hell, but I should always have my tea."

— Fyodor Dostoyevsky, Notes from Underground

REFERENCES

Bigelow. (2013). The History of Tea. Retrieved from Bigelow Tea. com: http://www.bigelowtea.com/universitea/history-of-tea. aspx

Duckler, D. (2013, February 8). Terroir and its Influence on the Flavor of Tea Part One. Retrieved June 18, 2013, from Verdant Tea.

Fuller, J. (2013). How Tea Works. Retrieved from How Stuff Works: http://science.howstuffworks.com/innovation/edible-innova-tions/tea1.htm

Gottatea Corp. (2010). History of Tea in the USA. Retrieved from Gottatea.com: http://www.gottatea.com/USA-tea-history

Heiss, M. L., & Heiss, R. J. (2010). The Tea Enthusiast's Handbook. New York: Ten Speed Press.

Heiss, R. J. (2008, March 20). Oxidation & Fermentation in Tea Manufacture. The Leaf.org, p. 5.

Imperial Tea Garden. (2003). Tea Grading. Retrieved from Imperial Tea Garden.com: http://www.imperialteagarden.com/teagrad-ing.html

Jenkins, M. (2010, May). The Forgotten Road. Retrieved from National Geographic Magazine: http://ngm.nationalgeo-graphic.com/print/2010/05/tea-horse-road/jenkins-text

Longbottom Coffee and Tea. (2009). Serving Tea: Milk, Lemon, Sugar or Plain? Retrieved from Longbottom Coffee and Tea: http://www.longbottomcoffee.com/ctu40.cfm

National Geographic. (2010). Lipton SustainabiliTea Q&A. Retrieved from Lipton SustainabiliTea: http://www.national-geographic.com/liptonsustainabilitea/qa.html

Pratt, J. N. (2002, March). The Original Book of Tea. Retrieved from Tea Muse Monthly Newsletter: http://www.teamuse.com/article_020302.html

RateTea.com. (2012, December 22). Oxidation of Tea. Retrieved from RateTea.Com: http://ratetea.com/topic/oxidation-of-tea/57/

RateTea.Com. (2013, April 9). Grades of Tea. Retrieved from Rate-Tea.com: http://ratetea.com/topic/grades-of-tea/17/

Rishi Tea. (2013). Yellow Tea. Retrieved from RIshi Tea: http://www.rishi-tea.com/category/yellow-tea

Rose, S. (2010). For All the Tea in China. New York: Penguin Group.

South African Rooibos Council. (2013). Rooibos FAQs. Retrieved from South African Rooibos Council: http://www.sarooibos.co.za/fact-file-mainmenu-46/faq-mainmenu-124

Stradley, L. (n.d.). History of Iced Tea and Sweet Tea. Retrieved from What's Cooking America: http://whatscookingamerica.net/History/IcedTeaHistory.htm

Tea USA. (2013). Tea Fact Sheet. Retrieved from Tea USA: http://www.teausa.com/14655/tea-fact-sheet

Teavana. (2013). History of Tea. Retrieved from Teavana: http://www.teavana.com/tea-info/history-of-tea

Teavana. (2013). Tea Info. Retrieved from Tea Info: http://www.teavana.com/tea-info/

Teavana. (2013). The Discovery of Tea. Retrieved from Teavana.
com: http://www.teavana.com/tea-info/discovery-of-tea

The East India Tea Company. (n.d.). The Story of Tea. Retrieved
from http://www.theeastindiacompany.com/index.php/24/
story-of-tea/?iframe=true&width=800&height=400&phpMyA
dmin=nuqL7SGlCRYlruX3W1VQYbLGvx1

United Kingdom Tea Council. (2013). History of the Tea Bag.
Retrieved from United Kingdom Tea Council: http://www.tea.
co.uk/the-history-of-the-tea-bag#invention

Wang, P. (2010, May 21). Oxidation of Tea 101. Retrieved June 18,
2013, from Teanmu Chaya

Teahouse Teahouse Stirrings: http://www.teanamu.com/2010/05/
oxidation-of-tea-101/

Yee, L. K. (2013, June 11). Tea's Wonderful History. Retrieved from
The Chinese Historical and Cultural Project: http://www.chcp.
org/tea.html

ENDNOTES

[1] (Tea USA, 2013)

[2] (Gottatea Corp, 2010)

[3] (Kuntze, 1996-2012)

[4] (Mair & Hoh, 2009)

[5] (Bigelow, 2013) (Teavana, 2013) (Yee, 2013)

[6] (Mair & Hoh, 2009, p27)

[7] (Jenkins, 2010) (Mair & Hoh, 2009), (Mair & Hoh, 2009, p41)

[8] (Jenkins, 2010) (Mair & Hoh, 2009) (Heiss & Heiss, 2010)

[9] (Mair & Hoh, 2009)

[10] (Pratt, 2002)

[11] (Pratt, 2002) (Mair & Hoh, 2009)

[12] (Sen Rikyū, 2014)

[13] (Japanese Tea Ceremony Equipment, 2011)

[14] (Mair & Hoh, 2009, p89-90)

[15] (Mair & Hoh, 2009)

[16] (Sen Rikyū, 2014)

[17] (Zen Stories of the Samuari - Sen No Rikyu; (Mair & Hoh, 2009)

[18] (Mair & Hoh, 2009)

[19] (Mair & Hoh, 2009)

[20] (Teavana, 2013)

[21] (Delaine, 2000)

[22] (Nagy, 2002)

[23] (Delaine, 2000; Mair & Hoh, 2009)

[24] (Teavana, 2013)

[25] (Bigelow, 2013) (Teavana, 2013)

[26] (Nagy, 2002)

[27] (Rose, 2010)

[28] (Rose, 2010)

[29] (Rose, 2010)

[30] (Gottatea Corp, 2010)

[31] (Fuller, 2013)

[32] (Gottatea Corp, 2010) (United Kingdom Tea Council, 2013)

[33] (Tea USA, 2013)

[34] (Gottatea Corp, 2010)

[35] (Stradley)

[36] (National Geographic, 2010)

[37] (Tea USA, 2013)

[38] (Duckler, 2013)

[39] (Heiss & Heiss, 2010)

[40] (Fuller, 2013)

[41] (Fuller, 2013) (RateTea.Com, 2013)

[42] (Heiss & Heiss, 2010)

[43] (RateTea.Com, 2013) (Heiss & Heiss, 2010) (Imperial Tea Garden, 2003)

[44] (Heiss R. J., 2008) (RateTea.com, 2012) (Wang, 2010)

[45] (Heiss & Heiss, 2010)

[46] (Heiss R. J., 2008)

[47] (Heiss & Heiss, 2010) (Teavana, 2013)

[48] (Heiss & Heiss, 2010) (Rishi Tea, 2013)

[49] (Heiss & Heiss, 2010) (Teavana, 2013)

[50] (Past Prime Ministers Charles Grey 2nd Earl Grey , 2014)

[51] (South African Rooibos Council, 2013)

[52] (Heiss & Heiss, 2010)

[53] (Longbottom Coffee and Tea, 2009)

[54] (Blended MEC, 2012)

[55] (Blended MEC, 2012) (Lininger, 2011)

[56] (Lininger, 2011)

[57] (The East India Tea Company)

IMAGE INFORMATION

Cover - Oolong

pg. viii - Pu–erh

pg. 3 - English Breakfast

pg. 4 - Pu-erh

pg. 6 - Yerba Mate Gourds

pg. 8–9 - Teapot and teacup

pg. 11 - A copper tea kettle

pg. 12 - A Yixing teapot and teacups

pg. 14 - Oolong

pg. 16–17 - Darjeeling

pg. 19 - White tea leaves

pg. 20 - Rooibos

pg. 23 - A pu–erh cake and tongs

pg. 24 - Genmaicha

pg. 25 - Oolong

pg. 27 - Darjeeling leaves

pg. 28 - Gunpowder green tea

pg. 30 - Yellow tea

pg. 32 - White tea

pg. 34 - Oolong tea leaves

pg. 36 - Earl Gray (with Lavender)

pg. 38 - Pu–erh

pg. 40 - Three assorted tisanes

pg. 42 - Rooibos

pg. 44 - Genmaicha

pg. 45 - Earl Gray (with Lavender)

pg. 47 - Earl Gray (with Lavender)

pg. 49 - Assorted tea equipment

pg. 50–51 - English Breakfast

pg. 52 - Wrapped pu–erh

pg. 54 - Afternoon tea and snacks

pg. 57 - A Yixing teapot and cups

pg. 59 - Oolong

pg. 95 - Various types of brewed tea leaves: white, green, black, and pu–erh

pg. 98 - Lapsang Souchong

pg. 100 - Assam

pg. 107 - English Breakfast

pg. 110 - English Breakfast

"We had a kettle; we let it leak:
Our not repairing made it worse.
We haven't had any tea for a week...
The bottom is out of the Universe."

— *Rudyard Kipling,*
The Collected Poems of Rudyard Kipling

ABOUT THE AUTHOR

http://www.viviancaethe.com/

Vivian Caethe's short stories and novellas have appeared in a variety of magazines and several anthologies. Her novella, *The Diamond City: The Adventures of Vernon Auldswell, Gentleman Explorer*, is published by Bold Strokes Books.

Inspired by growing up in the Land of Enchantment, she has been writing science fiction and fantasy since she was twelve.

An avid tea drinker, she is in the constant search for the perfect cup. She lives in Colorado with her husband.

ABOUT THE PHOTOGRAPHER

http://www.nuance-interactive.com

Never one to say "I don't know how", this has opened up opportunities for Amber Peter to design and build websites, create makeup art, film and edit videos, photograph events, design costumes, and now: beverage photography and book typesetting.

Drink the Tea

Made in the USA
Middletown, DE
27 May 2016